Songs For Koibe

Olivia Nguy

BookLeaf
Publishing

Presentation by *BookLeaf Publishing*

Web: www.bookleafpub.com

E-mail: info@bookleafpub.com

ISBN: 978-93-95784-87-0

First edition 2022

To and for my sweethearts Kolbe and Mr DW, with all my love. Special loving shout out to sweet Barkley and Nestor too. ❤

Prelude

Two destined souls
Laughter and music
Fireworks at night

A lemon tart, a coffee eclair
Jean Marc's crisp croissant

A Victorian sponge and some wedding cheese
and smoked bark follow on

Two hundred full moons
Four furry feet, two wiry ones
A Carrington to call home

A treasure map of memories
Totus tuus
The middle calls us on

A Song for Barkley

The joy of meeting you
And paws from furry friends
Your tiny being on my lap
Coming home
Resting your chin
Your smell made me your mama
A long time ago

My treat hiding Houdini
My hide and seek muppet foot friend
My bodyguard with suction feet
And bathroom sentry
The best greeter you could send

My winter blanket, flat face, crooked smile
Seeking belly rubs with cycling legs
My dining companion with longing eyes
And by foot past countless bends

Loving loyal Barkley
I love you without end

A Song for Nestor

Speckled little beauty
Warbles melodiously
Constant lively presence

Acrobatic Macgyver
High speed flyer
Nibbles leafy greens

Fiesty Nesty
Fearless friend
Hops and clings

Tongue flicking
Nesty kissing
The sweetest hair preening

Yearning

A whisper that it's time for you
Turns into a tug
A rope of indeterminate length
The sureness of you a shrug

As days and months and years go by
Our yearning more and more
A sinking heart with passing time without you at
our door

We hold on tight on to that rope
We pray you might come soon
Our destiny, our miracle
Borne from the fullest moon

Anticipation

Morning hope, anticipation
Tempered expectation
A long awaited line
Heart full, filled eyes
Tamed by the unknowns

Joy doubles as the news is shared
Our worries doubled too
We start to dream of life ahead
With you here in the room

Relief makes space for excitement
With the thumps of a steady heart
A waving hand there on the screen
We love you from the start

Carried

Tethered and nourished together
My precious little bump
My little sweetheart joey
We're a unit of two in one

With every day and adventure
Every whoosh and lilting step
May you know the depth of my love
The joy in my heart
And the wondrousness of the unfolding world

With all your kicks and flutters
To my days you bring delight
Your tiny little hiccups
Can you feel mama?
She holds you close and tight

DW Blessing

That you may be safe
That you have good health
That you be the kindest boy
That you will show courage to stand for what's
right
These are our hopes for you, our boy

That you will know love all through your life
That you'll know the touch of God
That you know how much you are loved by us
And leave your imprint of love in this world

These are our hopes for you sweetest boy
These are our hopes, our love

Maximilian Kolbe

He transformed the matter altogether for the old
Masters
While the children had missed the mark:
Martyrdom does not but simply run its course
Rather, it is a firmly active choice
Of love and courage,
Of conviction,
As a steadfast witness of truth and good and
right

While some torturer's horse may scratch its
innocent behind on a tree
Another can choose to unbridle itself
To vocalise
Or in its own quiet way
Tread to the light
And nuzzle its face against another

Birth Story

In your own perfect timing
You told me it's go time, mama go
2.30am my heart knew it
Though the build up was unexpectedly slow

Steady waves and surges
The pain would ebb and flow
We went about our merry day
Such that others didn't know

The pain picked up its pace
Til I couldn't take much more
12am we were at the hospital
I knelt on the delivery room floor

I held on to your father tight
With a cavewoman orca roar
You and I worked as a team
Until we could push no more

Thank goodness precious miracle
You came through at the last chance of a push
Things were starting to feel desperate
Til you sprung into my arms
Little Danger-Wolf

Origin

Remarkable innocence
Unblemished perfection
A touch of God, a glimpse of heaven

From a spark into my world
Precious miracle
Full circle to our destination

A split second into my arms
Leap and land
Forever in my heart

The First Hold

Surreal relief
Elation
Radiating joy
Gratitude like none other
Your slippery self unexpectedly in expectant
arms
Known and unknown at once

Sensing, feeling, connected
Instinct skin-to-skin
Golden hours gentle one
Safe and nestled within

The Dreamstone Cannery

Frankfurt fingers, starfish fists
Searching hands and face
A smile and chuckle off to sleep
Tiny chunky massaged feet

Young old man hair, tufts and swirls
Curious eyes so full of soul
Your button nose
Fullest cheeks
Your macarena pose

Your flailing arms
Your softest touch
Your gummy toothless smile

I'll bottle these warm in my heart
To hold time for a while

Mama's Mantra

Gentle murmur
Fierce protector
Tender my love for you

May you know it in the way I smooth your hair
Cradled in my arms
In the biggest smiles, the joy of day
And held close through the nights
In the gentle kiss of your forehead
I could eat your cheeks
And in my heartbeat against your ear as you sigh

Every good morning and good night
Every prayer that you're alright
In the hourly coos and sighs, a mantra
'Oh mummy loves you, my boy'

Here (Sweet dreams, goodnight)

Bathing in warmth
Emanating love
A perfect little fit between the crook of two arms

You gently knock
Then your arms wrap around

Presence in the moment
Your tiny hands cling on
Our shared hearth between bellies
Your even breath a song

Opening

How I've loved watching you
Unwrap the world
Little by little
A thousand shades of colour
The breadth of humanity
Gazing at bubbles in wonder

Undo the ribbons on
The smells of the bushland
Finding your feet
Beauty in music
Climbing mountainsides and peaks

Find the wonder in
The blanket of stars in the sky
The expanse of the ocean
The depths of love and friendship
And wildlife - totally wild

And delight in
The fun of play
The joy of baking
Undiscovered trails
Creative freedom

Food made with love
The wagging of a tail

Hi You! (A haiku about you)

A big smile spreads wide
Like the blue skies overhead
Bring forth warmth and joy

Midnight Orchestra

A symphony of snoring
One, two and three
Doggy, man, baby
Humming intimacy

Moore Reserve

Amongst the trees
The wind in our face
Gentle warmth of the sun cascades
The quiet hum of nature
And us, gazing upon creation
Delighting in each other

Home

Of love
Of rest and repose
Of safety
Of fun and games and laughter
Of hospitality
Of music
Of beauty
Of memories
Of chaos of life lived
Of welcome and friendship
Of companionship
Of where we belong
Home
Of family

Dear Kolbe

I can't wait to meet
You in 5 years
And in 10 and 20 too
And the man that you'll become
Yet still, don't grow too fast too soon

Pen to Paper

Here has always been
With you in my arms
Your warmth
Your gentleness
Your lashes
The smell of your tiny hands
Etched and treasured
Within these papers
And within memory, soul and heart